Original title:

Crystal Twilight

Copyright © 2024 Swan Charm
All rights reserved.

Author: Eliora Lumiste
ISBN HARDBACK: 978-9916-79-468-5
ISBN PAPERBACK: 978-9916-79-469-2
ISBN EBOOK: 978-9916-79-470-8

The Last Glimmer of Day

The sun dips low, a fiery glow,
Painting skies with hues aglow.
Whispers of night begin to weave,
A tender breath that few perceive.

Shadows stretch and softly creep,
As daylight bids the world to sleep.
Crickets chirp their evening song,
In nature's arms, we all belong.

Stars emerge, a diamond lace,
Each twinkle holds a secret place.
The last glimmer, a fleeting sight,
The end of day, the start of night.

Shimmering Whispers of the Evening Star

In twilight's embrace, the night unfurls,
Soft whispers dance in cosmic swirls.
The evening star begins her reign,
As shadows play on window panes.

Moonlit pathways, silvered dreams,
Underneath, the world softly gleams.
In the still of night, secrets hide,
With shimmering whispers, dreams collide.

Celestial glow, a gentle guide,
In the dark, where hopes reside.
The evening star, our silent muse,
In her light, we cannot lose.

Luster of Midnight's Kiss

Underneath the canopy of night,
The moon bestows her gentle light.
With luster bright, she lights the way,
Through shadows deep, where dreams can play.

Cool breezes stir, a fragrant sigh,
As midnight whispers sweetly nigh.
In silver beams, the world transforms,
With every heartbeat, passion warms.

Stars align, a tapestry wide,
In midnight's kiss, our hearts collide.
Lost in magic, time stands still,
As we chase dreams with heart and will.

Nautical Gleams of the Dusk

The ocean sighs at twilight's call,
Where horizon meets the sun's last sprawl.
Nautical gleams on waves do dance,
In mystery woven, we find romance.

Seagulls glide in the dusky air,
Carrying secrets we long to share.
Each ripple a story yet untold,
In shimmering whispers, brave and bold.

As day slips softly into night,
The sea reflects the evening light.
In this embrace, we feel alive,
With nautical dreams, our spirits thrive.

Dawn's Lament After the Glitter

The night has lost its glamour,
Stars whisper their goodbyes,
Shadows stretch to morning,
As daylight starts to rise.

Once the glitter dazzled bright,
Now it fades with the moon,
A sigh from the horizon,
Echoing nature's tune.

Colors blend in sorrow,
Painting the skies with grief,
Every ray a memory,
A short-lived, bright relief.

But dawn brings new beginnings,
With hopes that softly glow,
Though glitter fades to silence,
Life still finds ways to grow.

In the stillness of morning,
Fading echoes remain,
Reminding hearts of beauty,
In joy and also pain.

The Ebbing Radiance of Night

As the night begins to wane,
Stars lose their fiery dance,
Silhouettes of twilight fade,
In this fleeting glance.

Moonlight pours like silver,
Cascading soft and bright,
A gentle kiss of darkness,
Whispers through the night.

Yet shadows hold their secrets,
In corners vast and deep,
The radiance starts to ebb,
While weary hearts still sleep.

The dawn creeps in unhurried,
With fingers dipped in gold,
In its tender embrace,
Stories of night unfold.

Thus, light and dark entwine,
In an ever-changing play,
The ebbing of the radiance,
Marks the close of day.

Flickering Echoes Above the Horizon

Over the hills, light dances,
A flicker on the crest,
Whispers of the morning call,
Nature's gentle jest.

Echoes of a night well spent,
Softly kissed by dawn,
Colors breathe and shimmer,
As darkness is withdrawn.

A canvas of warm light paints,
The edges of the day,
In every hue and shade,
Life finds its playful way.

Yet in the flickering moments,
Lies a fleeting grace,
For time, like light, will vanish,
In the endless race.

So seize the hours that glimmer,
Make memories shine bright,
For flickering echoes linger,
Above the horizon's light.

Glistening Hues of Nightfall

Stars emerge in velvet skies,
Whispers float where silence lies.
Moonlight paints the world so bright,
Embracing all with soft delight.

Shadows dance on seas of gray,
Fading light slips far away.
Colors shift, the day departs,
Leaving traces on our hearts.

Night wraps us in a soothing shroud,
Crickets sing, the stars are proud.
Dreams awaken in the dark,
Illuminating every spark.

Glistening gems in heavens high,
Echoes of the night's soft sigh.
Nature breathes, a hushed refrain,
As darkness kisses earth again.

Twilight's Gentle Embrace

In shades of lavender and blue,
The world transforms, serene and new.
A tender kiss upon the hills,
As time unveils its gentle thrills.

Golden rays begin to fade,
Painting shadows like a braid.
Birds return to nests so warm,
Cradled close from every storm.

Twilight whispers secrets sweet,
Where day and night embrace and meet.
A bridge of light, a fleeting chance,
Nature's starlit, peaceful dance.

Every hue a story told,
Of moments lost and dreams of old.
In twilight's arms, we find our place,
Beneath the stars, in night's embrace.

Secrets Beneath the Glow

Beneath the moon's soft, watchful gaze,
A world unfolds in mystic ways.
Hidden paths where shadows creep,
And ancient promises do keep.

Lanterns sway on evening's breeze,
As laughter lingers among the trees.
Whispers shared in secret tones,
Reveal the heart's unguarded bones.

Every twinkle tells a tale,
Of love once lost, of dreams that sail.
The night conceals, yet gives a light,
To secrets woven into sight.

In glowing streets where memories blend,
Time wraps around, a faithful friend.
Underneath the cosmic show,
We forge the truths we long to know.

Afterglow's Resonance

As day bids farewell with a sigh,
Afterglow paints the evening sky.
Soft pastels in a warm embrace,
Tender moments we long to trace.

The sun dips low, a fiery ball,
Releasing echoes, a final call.
Colors merge in a tranquil stream,
Awakening life from our dream.

Fading light ignites our souls,
As the night quietly unfolds.
In every shade, a whisper clear,
Telling tales of those held dear.

The afterglow, a fleeting glance,
Invites us all to take a chance.
To find our place beneath the stars,
And cherish life's sweet memoirs.

Enchanted Hues of Dusk

The sun dips low in skies of gold,
As shadows stretch, the day grows old.
With every brush of twilight's hand,
A canvas blooms across the land.

Crimson rivers flow through the trees,
Whispering secrets in the breeze.
Stars awake to greet the night,
As dreams begin their gentle flight.

A hush descends upon the earth,
Where colors spark with hidden worth.
In this hour of soft embrace,
Magic flickers in every space.

The world transforms in fading light,
With shades of wonder, pure and bright.
Each heartbeat sings a sweet refrain,
Of beauty dwelling in the grain.

So linger here where dusk unfolds,
In enchanted hues both rich and bold.
Let the twilight cradle your soul,
In its embrace, we become whole.

Twilight's Glittering Embrace

In twilight's realm, the stars are born,
As day surrenders to the morn.
They sprinkle sparkles in the air,
Inviting dreams beyond compare.

The moon awakes, she softly glows,
With silver light that gently flows.
Her whispers dance on every breeze,
An ode to night, a tale to tease.

Reflections shimmer on the sea,
A reflection of eternity.
Within the waves, the magic sighs,
As twilight wraps the world in ties.

An endless sky of deepening hue,
With promises of nighttime's brew.
Each heartbeat echoes love's embrace,
In twilight's bright, enchanting space.

So let us find our way through night,
In glittering dreams, our souls take flight,
For in this hour, we are set free,
Entwined in all that we can be.

Luminescent Whispers

The night awakes with softest glow,
As secrets linger, spirits flow.
Whispers of light in shadows play,
Guiding us through the night's ballet.

Stars shimmer bright with tales untold,
In silver threads, the night enfold.
Each twinkle dances with pure grace,
Casting magic in this sacred space.

The breeze carries melodies sweet,
Of lullabies and heartbeats meet.
Faint echoes of forgotten dreams,
In luminescent, shining beams.

Through darkened paths where silence reigns,
A symphony eases all our pains.
Let starlight cradle weary minds,
And soothe the soul that hope still finds.

So wander deep in night's embrace,
Where whispers guide with gentle pace.
For in the dark, we find our way,
To the dawn's light, where hearts can stay.

Radiant Abyss

In the depths of night's embrace,
Lies a world of hidden grace.
The abyss glimmers with secrets bright,
Drawing dreams into its light.

Stars descend like scattered pearls,
Across the void where silence twirls.
Each moment holds a tale anew,
In the radiant dusk we pursue.

Echoes linger in the dark,
As shadows dance, igniting spark.
The cosmos paints with hues divine,
Connecting hearts in endless line.

Through the abyss, our spirits soar,
As brilliance opens every door.
We find our place among the night,
In radiant beauty, pure delight.

So let the darkness be our guide,
In this abyss, we will abide.
For in the depth, we learn to trust,
The radiant paths from stardust.

Glimmers of Dusk

In twilight's embrace, shadows play,
The world softens, drifts away.
Stars peek out, faint and shy,
As the sun bids a gentle goodbye.

Whispers of night begin to creep,
Secrets held in silence deep.
Moonlight dances on the stream,
Woven through the fabric of dreams.

Crickets sing in a hushed choir,
Branches sway, catching the fire.
Gentle breezes softly sigh,
While the lonesome owls call high.

Colors blend, like a painter's hue,
A canvas fresh with evening's dew.
Dusk unfolds its velvet cloak,
Unraveling tales the stars bespoke.

Time slips softly like a sigh,
In the quiet, the heart learns to fly.
Glimmers of dusk, a fleeting grace,
Holding night's magic in its embrace.

Ethereal Shimmers

In the hush of the night, they gleam,
Ethereal shimmers, like a dream.
Floating softly, pale and bright,
Guiding lost souls through the night.

They twinkle above, a cosmic dance,
Inviting all to take a chance.
Stories whispered in silver light,
Filling the void with pure delight.

Faint trails of luminescence glow,
Tracing paths where wild thoughts flow.
Hidden wonders start to appear,
In each flicker, a gentle cheer.

Woven threads of starlit lace,
Wrap the world in warm embrace.
With every flash, hope ignites,
Lighting up the canvas of nights.

Ethereal shimmers, soft and rare,
Speak of magic found everywhere.
In every glance, a mystery unfolds,
Whispers of tales waiting to be told.

The Veil of Evening

The veil of evening drapes the land,
With colors brushed by a painter's hand.
Soft hues melt into twilight's grace,
Time slows down in this sacred space.

Whispers float on a silken breeze,
Carrying secrets through the trees.
Stars awaken, one by one,
As the day yields to the night begun.

Clouds gather, like dreams in flight,
Veiling the remnants of fading light.
Moon rises slowly, proud and bright,
Draping shadows in silver light.

Laughter fades, giving way to sighs,
As the world dons its dusk disguise.
Candle flames flicker, thin and wispy,
Creating reflections that feel so misty.

The veil of evening, soft and true,
Embraces the heartbeat, old and new.
In its folds, forgotten names,
And whispered hopes, like flickering flames.

Luminous Phantoms

Through the mist, they silently glide,
Luminous phantoms, with nowhere to hide.
Gentle glows in the shadowed night,
Casting visions of fleeting light.

Echoes of laughter linger near,
Haunting whispers only we hear.
Phantoms of dreams drift in the air,
Shaping moments beyond compare.

Ghostly figures swirl and sway,
Guiding lost hearts along the way.
With each twinkle, a story unfolds,
Of passions burning, and love untold.

In moonbeams bright, they find their dance,
Casting spells with a wistful glance.
Through the darkness, they softly roam,
Finding solace in the night's warm home.

Luminous phantoms, soft and shy,
Soon return to the midnight sky.
Yet in their wake, a spark remains,
A reminder of love that still sustains.

Moonlit Daubs of Light

In the stillness of night,
Whispers of silver drift,
Painting the world in calm,
Under the moon's soft lift.

Stars twinkle like gems,
Scattering dreams on the ground,
A dance of celestial hues,
In silence, magic is found.

Shadows weave through the trees,
A tapestry of delight,
Each branch a story told,
Under the moon's watchful light.

Ripples on the mirror lake,
Reflecting the glowing sphere,
Nature's breath takes a pause,
In the stillness, we hear.

As dawn teeters on the edge,
The light begins to break,
Yet the memory lingers still,
Of the beauty we awake.

A Palette of Starlit Fantasies

A canvas brushed with dreams,
In colors bold and bright,
Each star a stroke of wonder,
In the deep velvet night.

Glimmers of cosmic tales,
Dancing in the vast expanse,
Inviting us to wander,
In a celestial trance.

Whispers of ancient lore,
Echo through the skies,
The night, a sweet embrace,
Where imagination flies.

Each constellation glows,
A story carved in time,
Drawing paths in the dark,
With an artist's silent rhyme.

Beneath this painted dome,
We find our hearts take flight,
In the palette of the stars,
We dream, we love, we write.

The Twinkle of Dusk's Melody

As day bids its sweet goodbye,
The twilight starts to play,
A symphony of colors,
As night takes the day away.

Gentle notes of the breeze,
Carry secrets from afar,
Every breath a soft surrender,
To the rising evening star.

A chorus of shadowed forms,
Begin to softly dance,
While whispers of dusk's beauty,
Invite us to take a chance.

Under the fading light,
Time seems to slow its race,
In the melody of dusk,
We find a warm embrace.

Each moment gently glows,
With the promise of the night,
In the twinkle of dusk's song,
Our souls take their flight.

Glinting Reveries of the Evening Light

In the hush of twilight's glow,
Dreams twinkle like the stars,
Painting glinting reveries,
From Jupiter to Mars.

The horizon spills with gold,
A ribbon 'round the sky,
With every shade of sunset,
The day bids a sweet bye.

Silhouettes stretch and yawn,
In the fading light we stand,
Memory lingers like whispers,
In the glow's gentle hand.

As night wraps us in calm,
A quilt stitched from the day,
We gather all our dreams,
In the night's vast array.

Each twinkle, a promise made,
In the canvas of the night,
Glinting reveries shimmer,
In the world's soft delight.

The Last Breath of Day

As sun dips low, the sky ignites,
With hues of gold and crimson lights.
Whispers of night begin to dance,
In the twilight's gentle glance.

Stars awaken, soft and bright,
In the embrace of coming night.
The world exhales, a tranquil sigh,
As the day bids sweet goodbye.

Shadows stretch with quiet grace,
Nature wears a dimmed embrace.
Colors fade, the stars confer,
In the hush, the dreams occur.

Moonrise paints the calmest scene,
A tapestry of soft, serene.
In the stillness, hearts will find,
The beauty left by day behind.

With every breath, a story weaves,
Of the memories that night leaves.
So let the darkness softly play,
In the last breath of fading day.

Enchanted Evening's Serenade

Underneath the velvet sky,
Fireflies twinkle, passing by.
The nightingale starts to sing,
Her melody, a soothing thing.

Moonlight spills on silver streams,
Crickets hum the sweetest dreams.
A gentle breeze whispers low,
Sharing secrets only they know.

Soft petals fall from blossoms fair,
Filling the night with a fragrant air.
Laughter lingers, dances round,
In this magic, joy is found.

Shadows sway in rhythm slow,
As stars above begin to glow.
Together in this sacred space,
Every heart finds its own place.

With each note, the night unfolds,
A serenade of stories told.
In the warmth of evening's bliss,
We find the peace in every kiss.

Flickers in the Gloom

In the stillness, shadows creep,
Secrets hidden, silence deep.
Every corner, whispers loom,
Ghostly echoes in the gloom.

Flickers of a distant flame,
Bringing light, yet still the same.
Shapes emerge from darkened walls,
Shivering as the night enthralls.

Through the mist, a figure glides,
In the dark where mystery hides.
A fleeting thought, a vision passed,
In the quiet, thoughts are cast.

Candles flicker, soft and bright,
Guiding souls through endless night.
In the gloom where fears reside,
Hope ignites, inviting pride.

As dawn breaks, the shadows flee,
In the light, we come to see.
What once felt lost, we will reclaim,
No longer bound by ancient shame.

The Cosmic Canvas

With every star, a story spun,
In the vastness, journeys run.
Nebulas in hues divine,
Sketching dreams in endless line.

Galaxies swirl in graceful arcs,
An artist's touch, the heaven's sparks.
Wonders dance in cosmic flow,
As quiet whispers start to grow.

Time and space, a woven thread,
Connections made with what is said.
In the silence, truths collide,
Human hearts will not divide.

Planets twirl in endless play,
In the night, they find their way.
Shooting stars ignite the night,
Bringing forth a fleeting light.

Each moment captured in the dark,
A constellation's hidden mark.
On this canvas, wide and free,
The universe sings poetry.

Whispered Illuminations

In twilight's grasp, we softly tread,
Where whispers dance, and dreams are fed.
Soft beams flicker, guiding the way,
Illuminating what words can't say.

Through tangled woods, the secrets weave,
In rustling leaves, we pause, believe.
A gentle sigh, the night expands,
Hope cradled close in shimmering bands.

Stars spill forth in silver streams,
Painting the sky with fragile dreams.
The moon, a guardian, stands so bright,
Watching over hearts, igniting light.

In every shadow, a story lies,
Whispered truths beneath the skies.
Together we walk, hand in hand,
In whispered illuminations, we stand.

The Light Between Worlds

A bridge of dawn, the night must yield,
Where shadows merge, and truths are healed.
In golden hues, a moment's grace,
We find our way, we seek a space.

Between the realms, where silence curates,
Time pauses softly, fear abates.
Reflections glisten, hopes alive,
In the light between, we learn to thrive.

Memories linger like painted skies,
With every heartbeat, laughter flies.
A dance of colors, fading and bright,
The souls connect in shared delight.

Stepping forth through veils so thin,
A journey starts as shadows spin.
With love as our compass, we embark,
To chase our dreams, igniting the spark.

Shimmering Shadows

In twilight's haze, the shadows creep,
Whispers fold, secrets keep.
Beneath the stars, they twist and twine,
In shimmering shades, our fates align.

Each flicker fades, yet holds a thrill,
Silent echoes, hearts to fill.
Among the dusk, where fears are laid,
Shimmering shadows, a serenade.

Through corridors of night we roam,
With every step, we find a home.
In glimmers faint, old tales revive,
In shimmering shades, we come alive.

Embracing twilight's soft embrace,
We dance with time, and find our grace.
In every shroud of silken night,
Shimmering shadows reveal the light.

Fragments of a Fading Day

As sunlight wanes, the colors blend,
Whispers of dusk, a gentle end.
In echoes soft, the night unfurls,
Fragments lost in a world of swirls.

Crimson skies bleed into blue,
A fleeting moment, precious and true.
With every breath, the day withdraws,
Leaving traces of its gentle cause.

The horizon blushes, shadows creep,
A lullaby for the world asleep.
Cascading hues like dreams in flight,
Fragments blossom in soft twilight.

In the quiet hush of fading glow,
We gather memories, feelings flow.
In the tapestry of night's embrace,
We find our peace, a sacred space.

Symphony of Shadows

Whispers dance in moonlit hours,
Fingers trace the night's dark flowers.
Echoes blend in soft embrace,
Silent song fills empty space.

Winds caress the ancient trees,
Carrying tales on gentle breeze.
Stars above, a watchful choir,
Kindling hearts with hidden fire.

Shadows stretch with like a sigh,
Painting dreams against the sky.
Lost in thoughts that softly roam,
In the dark, we find our home.

Beauty winks from starry seams,
Gliding through our fragile dreams.
Each moment softly drapes,
In the night, the soul escapes.

Rivers murmur secrets low,
Carrying whispers of the doe.
Nature hums with tender grace,
In this realm, we find our place.

Echoes in Soft Luminescence

Flickers of light in the silent mist,
Gentle glow that can't be missed.
Dancing particles in the air,
Whispers of magic everywhere.

The moon smiles on tranquil seas,
Caressing night with quiet ease.
Each shimmer holds a secret tale,
Carried softly on the gale.

Footprints left on silver sand,
Guided by a tender hand.
Nature's breath, a lullaby,
Sings to stars that drift on high.

Echoes reverberate through time,
Songs of earth, a sacred rhyme.
In the silence, souls unite,
Wrapped within this warm twilight.

Shadows blend with golden light,
Endless whispers greet the night.
Every heartbeat in the air,
A reminder that love is rare.

The Twilight Chorus

As the sun dips below the hill,
Nature pauses, quiet, still.
Cicadas join in twilight's tune,
A serenade that ends too soon.

Each note soft like a lover's sigh,
Drifting gently through the sky.
Stars awaken, one by one,
Filling darkness with the sun.

Moonlight kisses every tree,
Painting shadows tenderly.
In this dusk, our spirits blend,
Where darkness meets the day's sweet end.

A chorus rises, wild and true,
With echoes of the evening dew.
Breath of night, our hearts align,
In the twilight, we intertwine.

Voices rise, a symphony,
Sharing dreams of what could be.
In the gloam, we find our song,
In the dark, where we belong.

Embrace of the Gloaming

In the fold of evening's glow,
Softly whispers come and go.
Crickets chirp their lullabies,
Beneath the vast and starry skies.

The world slips into twilight's arms,
Wrapped in nature's gentle charms.
Every shadow, a friend to keep,
In this moment, silence deep.

Hills blush in the setting sun,
As day's bright race is finally done.
The breeze hums with an ancient grace,
In the gloaming, we find our place.

Memories gather like fading light,
Whispers of love fill the night.
As stars uncover their hidden dreams,
In this hour, all is as it seems.

Each heartbeat drifts with gentle ease,
Carried softly by the breeze.
Together, in this sacred space,
We celebrate the night's embrace.

The Last Flicker of Daylight

The sun dips low in the sky,
Casting shadows that sigh.
Whispers of warmth drift away,
As night prepares to play.

Colors bleed into the night,
Fading softly from sight.
Birds hush in their flight path,
Nature's calm aftermath.

A final gleam, golden bright,
Before surrendering light.
Stars stir from their slumber,
In this quiet encumber.

The moon rises, bold and round,
In dreams, peace is found.
The last flicker fades fast,
While memories are cast.

With twilight's gentle hand,
The world stirs, carefully planned.
In the stillness, we dwell,
A story only time will tell.

Glistening Echoes of Dusk

The sky blushes with a glow,
Soft whispers begin to flow.
Each star awakes with grace,
In the dusk's warm embrace.

Ripples dance on the lake,
With every shimmer, heartache.
Moonbeams cast their gentle nets,
Catch our tangled silhouettes.

As shadows stretch and sigh,
Nightfall's curtain draws nigh.
Echoes of laughter play,
In the gloaming's soft sway.

The world dons a silver dress,
Wrapped in night's soft caress.
Time hums a lullaby sweet,
As dusk and dreams softly meet.

Glistening moments like dew,
Bringing memories anew.
In twilight's tender glow,
Our secrets begin to flow.

Quicksilver Dreams at Nightfall

In the realm where shadows blend,
Night invites us to transcend.
Quicksilver dreams take flight,
Borrows stars from the night.

Visions swirl in muted shades,
Softly drawn where hope pervades.
A canvas stretched wide and free,
Crafting tales of mystery.

Beneath a sky, deep and vast,
Whispers call from the past.
Each dream beckons, renewed,
In the silence, stories brood.

With each heartbeat, worlds collide,
In this mystic night tide.
Fleeting moments entwine,
In the twinkling divine.

Quicksilver dances like fire,
Igniting the heart's desire.
At nightfall, we learn to see,
The grace of what can be.

Silhouettes Bathing in Dazzle

In the glow of twilight's kiss,
Silhouettes emerge from bliss.
Dancing lines against the flame,
An ethereal game.

Each figure sways, whispers soft,
In the haze of dreams aloft.
Bathing in radiant light,
Chasing shadows through the night.

Mysteries in still air gleam,
As hearts wander in a dream.
Journeying through unseen lanes,
Silent joy in tangled chains.

Moments flicker like the stars,
Healing all our hidden scars.
Together, they weave and spin,
As the night prepares to begin.

Silhouettes painted with grace,
Timeless beauty in this space.
Lost in the dazzle, we become,
Part of the night's gentle hum.

The Luminous Eclipse

In shadows deep, the light withdraws,
The moon in hush, a silent cause.
Stars blink awake, in cosmic play,
As day gives way to night's ballet.

Veils of darkness weave and wend,
As twilight dreams begin to blend.
The world holds breath, a whispered sigh,
In the embrace of the inked sky.

A fleeting dance, a stellar sight,
The sun bids fare, the moon takes flight.
Glimmers caught in astral streams,
A moment's pause, where starlight beams.

As time stands still, beneath this shroud,
Hearts gather close; the night is proud.
Eclipsed in wonder, lost in time,
In silence wrapped, a fleeting rhyme.

Then dawn must break, the shadows flee,
The world returns to light carefree.
Yet in the mind, the mark remains,
A luminous tale where magic reigns.

Ethereal Glow at Dusk

As the sun dips low, the sky ignites,
With hues of pink, and soft delights.
Nature breathes in a calm embrace,
Ethereal glow, a fleeting grace.

Birds sing sweetly, their songs unwind,
In gentle whispers, the day resigned.
Clouds dance softly, in twilight's kiss,
Moments captured, a tranquil bliss.

The horizon blurs, where dreams reside,
In the fading light, the stars confide.
Secrets painted in pastel skies,
As day departs, the night complies.

Shadows stretch, as the chill descends,
With every heartbeat, the magic bends.
In the dusk's embrace, the world feels new,
An ethereal glow, a vibrant view.

Hold tight to dusk, let your spirit soar,
In the softening light, find so much more.
For in this hour, the heart can see,
The beauty wrapped in infinity.

Celestial Drizzle

A gentle rain of stardust falls,
Across the night, in whispered calls.
Each drop a wish, a spark divine,
In celestial peace, hearts intertwine.

The moonlight glistens on silver streams,
Reflecting hopes, and tender dreams.
The world washed clean in night's soft glow,
As cosmic wonders begin to flow.

Floating through the silence, we crave,
The rhythms of the night, so brave.
Galaxies twirl in the velvet sky,
As we watch the universe drift by.

The music of the spheres resounds,
In harmony, the night abounds.
Stars blink like jewels in a velvet gown,
A celestial dance, heavenward bound.

In this drizzle, let spirits rise,
In the cosmic ballet, we'll find our ties.
With every drop, the heart will beat,
In a swirl of dreams, we are complete.

Reflective Hues of Night

As darkness falls, the canvas glows,
With hues of night that softly flows.
Mirrors of stars on a tranquil sea,
Reflective whispers, wild and free.

Glimmers catch in the eye's embrace,
A calmness spreads, in this vast space.
Each twinkle tells a story old,
In the tapestry of night, bold.

The shadows play, a mystic dance,
Inviting all to take a chance.
In whispered tones, the cosmos speaks,
In the night's embrace, our spirit seeks.

Colors merge in the silent air,
Painting dreams that linger everywhere.
With every breath, the heart ignites,
In the reflective hues of starry nights.

So let us wander, hand in hand,
Through the wonders where magic stands.
In the night's arms, our fears take flight,
In reflective hues, we find our light.

The Whispering Light

In the stillness of dawn's breath,
A whisper trails through the trees,
Gentle rays of golden warmth,
Caressing leaves with soft ease.

Shadows dance on the cool ground,
As birds break into sweet song,
The world awakens all around,
To a melody soft and strong.

Morning dew clings to petals,
Glistening like diamonds bright,
Nature's jewels tell stories,
Of dreams in the whispering light.

Every hue begins to shimmer,
As colors blend and entwine,
A canvas of daybreak blooms,
In the warmth of the sun's design.

Listen close to the whispers,
For secrets that nature imparts,
In the light that paints the world,
And stirs the depths of our hearts.

Dance of the Dusk Fairies

When twilight falls with soft grace,
The fairies twirl in the night,
With whispering wings like soft lace,
They weave through shadows in flight.

Stars blink softly above them,
As the moon starts to glow bright,
In this realm where dreams begin,
They dance in the silver light.

Laughter echoes through the trees,
As they sprinkle their stardust fair,
Creating spells on the breeze,
In a world beyond all compare.

Their laughter weaves tales untold,
As the night wraps us in its embrace,
Magic glimmers, pure as gold,
In the flicker of each fairy's grace.

With every twirl, they invite,
Join the dance, let worries cease,
For in this moment of light,
We find our hearts' gentle peace.

Where Stars Begin to Shine

In the deep of the velvet night,
Stars awaken, one by one,
They flicker softly with delight,
A celestial dance has begun.

Whispers of dreams ride the air,
Guiding wishes on their flight,
Hope ignites in the stillness there,
Where stars begin to shine so bright.

Constellations weave their tales,
Of heroes, love, and ancient quests,
Their light across the dark sails,
Inviting all to find their rests.

Gaze up high, the universe calls,
As hearts are lifted to the sky,
In the shimmer, our spirit thralls,
Where every lost dream can fly.

Here in the night's soft embrace,
We are part of a grand design,
In the stillness, we find our place,
Where wonders and stars intertwine.

Beneath the Twilight Veil

Beneath the twilight's gentle veil,
The world dissolves into hues,
With whispers soft, the shadows sail,
As daylight bids its fond adieus.

Crickets chirp their evening song,
While fireflies dot the dark,
In this moment, we belong,
As nature glows with a spark.

The sky blushes in shades of pink,
As stars start to peek and play,
In silence, we sip, and think,
Of the magic in the fray.

Cool breezes dance through the night,
Carrying dreams on their wings,
In the embrace of fading light,
The heart discovers what it sings.

So let us linger, hand in hand,
As night wraps us in a shawl,
Beneath this twilight wonderland,
We find the beauty in it all.

Chasing Dusk

The sun dips low, a fiery ball,
Whispers fade as shadows call.
Colors blend in soft embrace,
Night draws near with gentle grace.

Crickets sing in rhythmic tune,
Stars awaken, one by one,
The world slows, a tender hush,
In the twilight, dreams all rush.

With every breath, the day departs,
A fleeting dance of light and arts,
Golden hues give way to gray,
Chasing dusk, we lose our way.

The sky wears velvet, deep and wide,
As moonlight takes the sun's great ride.
Soft winds carry secrets tight,
In the stillness of the night.

Embrace the dusk, let shadows creep,
In twilight's arms, we find our sleep.
Each star above, a distant guide,
In chasing dusk, we coincide.

Beyond the Fading Horizon

Where the sky kisses the sea,
Mysteries swirl, wild and free.
Beyond the fading, dreams take flight,
In whispers soft, they seek the light.

Waves crash down with foamy grace,
Footprints linger, time won't chase.
The sun bows low, the colors fuse,
Each moment breathes, we cannot choose.

Clouds drift slowly overhead,
Carrying secrets left unsaid.
A journey calls, it beckons brave,
Beyond horizons, our souls to save.

With every step, horizons shift,
A gift of truth, beyond the rift.
In the stillness, hearts align,
A world uncharted, yet divine.

As twilight wraps the vibrant sky,
Fear not to spread your wings and fly.
For beyond the fading, we will find,
Eternal wonders, intertwined.

Glowing Embers of Night

In the quiet, embers glow,
Softly lighting shadows low.
Each flicker tells a tale of old,
Of warmth and dreams, both brave and bold.

The moon dangles like a charm,
Her gentle light a soothing balm.
Stars like lanterns dance above,
In the night, we feel the love.

Whispers linger in the air,
Secrets shared with those who dare.
To gaze upon the velvet sky,
And dream of journeys yet to fly.

Through glowing embers, wisdom gleams,
In night's embrace, we find our dreams.
The world transforms in shadows bright,
Guided softly by the night.

So let us cozy by the fire,
With hopeful hearts and deep desire.
For every ember, a story lies,
Glowing softly, under starlit skies.

The Enigma of Twilight's Glow

Beneath the arch of twilight's hue,
An enigma swirls in shades of blue.
Mysteries dance where shadows play,
In the glow, the world turns gray.

Colors merge, a painter's scheme,
Reality shifts, like a dream.
As day retreats and night awakes,
A symphony of silence breaks.

In the wonder of fading light,
We ponder truth, we seek the right.
Whispers linger of what has been,
In twilight's glow, we search within.

Each heartbeat echoes, time reveals,
The secrets that the dusk conceals.
In this moment, we feel at peace,
With every breath, a soul's release.

As stars ignite, the night begins,
With gentle sighs, our journey spins.
In twilight's embrace, we find our way,
The enigma of night guides our stay.

Veils of Glistening Night

The stars above whisper sweet delight,
As shadows weave through the velvet night.
Moonbeams dance on the silken ground,
Secrets of dusk in silence found.

Whispers of wind stir the cool air,
While dreams take flight without a care.
A silhouette graced by soft light,
Cloaked in the veils of glistening night.

Crickets sing their melodic tune,
As fireflies blink beneath the moon.
Nature's chorus in harmony flows,
Wrapped in the magic that twilight knows.

The world is hushed, hearts gently sway,
In the embrace of the fading day.
Stars like diamonds, brightly ignite,
Within the realm of the quiet night.

Beneath the vastness, dreams take flight,
Carried away on the winds of night.
Veils of darkness softly enfold,
A story of whispers waiting to be told.

The Aurora Beneath the Surface

Beneath the waves, colors arise,
A hidden glow, a painter's guise.
The depths hold tales of ages past,
In luminous strokes, shadows cast.

Coral reefs whisper secrets shy,
Dancing fish in vibrant dye.
Hidden realms where dreams come true,
In currents swirling, life anew.

Sunlight trickles through the deep,
Awakening creatures from their sleep.
The ocean's heart, a canvas wide,
Painted by tides that ebb and glide.

A symphony of life, softly heard,
In the silence where dreams are stirred.
Nature's palette, rich and bright,
The aurora gleams in ethereal light.

In the embrace of the ocean's tear,
Mysteries dance, inviting cheer.
Beneath the waves, magic flows,
In vibrant hues, the world glows.

Twilight Shines through Glass

In windows framed with gentle light,
Twilight spills in, soft and bright.
Casting shadows on the floor,
A moment lost, forevermore.

Golden hues touch every pane,
Kissing the day as night begins to reign.
Reflections bend in the fading glow,
The stories that only silence knows.

Fractured rays in colors blend,
A fleeting glimpse where dreams descend.
Each shard of light a whispered sigh,
As stars awaken in the sky.

The world outside begins to fade,
As twilight's beauty is softly laid.
In glassy frames, memories twine,
Moments captured, pure and divine.

With every gaze, a narrative spins,
As night adorns with joyful hymns.
Twilight whispers through the glass,
An eternal moment, destined to pass.

A Celestial Dance of Reflections

Stars pirouette in the cosmic sea,
Writing stories of you and me.
Galaxies swirl in a grand ballet,
As night unfolds the dreams we play.

Comets trail with a fiery grace,
A fleeting glimpse, a brave embrace.
Orbits trace paths of divine design,
In the silence where shadows entwine.

From distant worlds, echoes resound,
Harmony in the vastness found.
Nebulae bloom in colors bold,
A tapestry of wonders untold.

With every twinkle and distant call,
The universe beckons, inviting all.
A celestial dance to the heart's delight,
As reflections shimmer in the night.

In the cosmic waltz, we spin and sway,
Caught in the magic, forever to stay.
Together we dream, in eternity's trance,
In a celestial dance, a timeless romance.

Celestial Harmony

Stars above in silent grace,
Waves of light they softly trace.
In the night, dreams intertwine,
Whispers sweet, a love divine.

Galaxies in endless dance,
Echoes of a cosmic chance.
Fading worlds, a gentle sigh,
Connected by the endless sky.

Moons that shine with silver beams,
Holding tight our fleeting dreams.
In their glow, our hearts take flight,
Boundless love in shadowed night.

Harmony in every star,
Guides us, no matter how far.
In the vastness, find our place,
Eternity in soft embrace.

Celestial whispers fill the air,
Tales of love beyond compare.
In this night, together be,
Lost in sweet eternity.

Evening's Enchantment

Beneath the dusk, the world turns slow,
Colors blend in a vibrant glow.
Gentle breezes start to sway,
As light ebbs with the fading day.

Crickets sing their nightly song,
In their chorus, we belong.
Fireflies dance in fleeting flight,
Nature's magic in the night.

Sleepless dreams begin to rise,
Painting patterns in our skies.
Every shadow softly plays,
Telling tales of bygone days.

Stars awaken, one by one,
Hoping dreams have just begun.
In the silence, hearts will mend,
Evening's magic knows no end.

Wrapped in twilight's warm embrace,
We find solace, seek our place.
With each pulse, the night will start,
Evening's enchantment fills the heart.

Veiled in Soft Luminescence

Fog rolls in, a whispered shroud,
Hiding secrets, soft and proud.
In the stillness, shadows blend,
Embracing all that night can send.

Moonlight dances on the dew,
Brushes soft, a silver view.
Nature's breath, a calming hymn,
Guides the night through shadows dim.

Glimmers tease the eye's delight,
Veiled in soft luminescent light.
Every branch and leaf awakes,
As the mystic silence quakes.

Voices lost within the haze,
Murmurs of forgotten days.
In this space where dreams collide,
Hope and wonder set aside.

Veiled in magic, pure and bright,
Colors shift in soft twilight.
In the gloom, we find our way,
Guided by the moon's soft ray.

Ribbons of Twilight

Whispers of a fleeting day,
Colors blend in soft array.
Shadows stretch as sun dips low,
Painting skies with evening glow.

Ribbons wrap the world in light,
Stitching dreams in darkening night.
Each horizon softly bends,
As daylight yields, the night ascends.

Stars emerge like scattered seeds,
Sowing hope where silence feeds.
In the twilight's tender hold,
Stories waiting to be told.

Footsteps quiet on the ground,
In the dusk, a peaceful sound.
Nature breathes a gentle sigh,
As time drifts while moments fly.

Wrapped in ribbons, soft and wide,
We wander with the evening tide.
In the dusk, we find our grace,
Ribbons of twilight's warm embrace.

A Cascade of Dusk's Colors

Soft whispers blend with golden rays,
As evening dances, night gently sways.
A palette spills, hues rich and bright,
Embracing the hush that follows the light.

Crimson clouds float, kissed by the breeze,
While shadows unfurl beneath the trees.
A tapestry woven in violet threads,
The sun bids farewell as darkness spreads.

Glimmers of hope in fading gray,
Stars begin to peek, they've come out to play.
The world slows down, wrapped in soft sighs,
As dusk paints its canvas across the skies.

Reflections flicker on water's surface,
Beneath the sky's vast, majestic wide verses.
Each moment a brushstroke, a fleeting delight,
In the cascade of all that awaits the night.

With gentle rhythm, twilight enthralls,
Nature's serenade in silken sprawls.
A cascade of dusk left to unfold,
In shades of wonder and stories untold.

The Illume of Ethereal Dreams

In the realm where shadows gleam,
A quiet whisper stirs the dream.
Lights like wings, flutter and glide,
In a world where wonders abide.

Softly, the moon begins to rise,
Casting silver on tranquil skies.
Illuminating paths yet trod,
With a gentle grace, an ethereal nod.

Each star a tale, a wish in flight,
A beacon of hope in the velvet night.
In dreams we dance on starlit streams,
Chasing the glow of our deepest dreams.

Whispers of time in delicate layers,
Carried on soft, celestial prayers.
Harmonies echo in softest sighs,
As the illume of magic silently flies.

Awake, we gather the remnants so bright,
Holding the glow of each wondrous night.
In the depths of our hearts, they forever gleam,
The memories swirled in ethereal dreams.

Serenade of Shimmering Lights

Beneath the veil of a twilight cloak,
Flickering jewels spark and evoke.
A serenade weaves through the air,
And lights join together in love and care.

Soft candles sway in the evening breeze,
Sharing secrets with rustling leaves.
Twinkling songs in a melodious flight,
Filling the corners of the emerging night.

A dance of colors, gold and blue,
Each shimmer reflects a heart's truth.
In the embrace of the night sky's grace,
The serenade finds its timeless place.

Whispers of laughter, a world so bright,
Brought to life by the shimmering light.
Together they twirl in a radiant play,
Resonating joy as they drift away.

When the darkness unfolds like a dream,
The lights keep flickering, a vibrant beam.
In hearts they linger, a cherished sight,
Forever alive in the serenade of lights.

Evening's Glistening Choreography

Veils of dusk with a touch of grace,
Reveal the night in a soft embrace.
Each twinkle dances, a ballet divine,
In evening's glimmering, sacred design.

Stars pirouette in the velvet sky,
While moonbeams wink as they pass by.
A choreography that stirs the soul,
In the theater where shadows roll.

Soft breezes waltz through branches and leaves,
Sending shivers like whispered reprieves.
The world unfolds in graceful spins,
As evening invites the dance to begin.

Crickets provide a gentle score,
While fireflies flicker on the forest floor.
Step by step, the night reveals,
A glistening magic that quietly heals.

In the normal of night, the extraordinary flows,
As nature showcases her luminous shows.
A testament to beauty, a nightly decree,
In evening's choreography, wild and free.

Aurora's Silent Reverie

In whispers soft, the night unfolds,
The stars reflect in silver gold.
A gentle hush envelops all,
As shadows dance, and nightbirds call.

Dreams drift lightly on the breeze,
Embracing thoughts, like rustling leaves.
A tapestry of hope takes flight,
Through shades of deep and twinkling light.

The dawn awaits, a palette bright,
Yet here, we linger in the night.
With velvet hues and solemn grace,
Aurora's whispers leave no trace.

In silence lost, the heart perceives,
The beauty wrapped in twilight eaves.
Each fading star a quiet tune,
A serenade to the coming moon.

So let us sit and dream awhile,
Embraced in night's enchanting smile.
For every moment softly shared,
Is one that blooms, a love declared.

Fading Echoes of Light

The sunset bleeds in shades of red,
Whispers linger, once loudly spread.
Ghosts of laughter float through the air,
A symphony of dreams laid bare.

In quietude, the colors blend,
While daylight bids a soft good friend.
Secrets murmur in twilight's glow,
As shadows stretch, their tales to sow.

Each heartbeat pulses, a gentle sigh,
As the sun dips low, bidding goodbye.
The stars begin their ancient play,
In silence, night steals light away.

The echoes fade, yet still they cling,
To memories of the joys they bring.
In softest hums that fill the night,
Resonates the fading light.

With every dusk, a canvas new,
Where dreams awaken, bright and true.
In the darkness, hopes align,
Fading echoes, forever shine.

Silken Skies

Above, a sea of endless blue,
In silken folds, the dreams imbue.
A gentle breeze, it whispers soft,
As clouds amble, aloft, aloft.

Golden rays break through the haze,
A dance of light, a chromatic blaze.
Each sunbeam weaves with sweet caress,
Across the vastness, they coalesce.

In twilight's reach, the colors meld,
The day's sweet tales yet to be held.
As dusk descends, a tapestry,
Of amber threads, and mystery.

Like satin draped across the sky,
In hues of love, dreams flutter by.
With every shimmer and every gleam,
The world ignites a waking dream.

So let us stand, hearts open wide,
Beneath the silken, starry tide.
For in each glance, and every sigh,
Lives the wonder of the sky.

A Dance of Fading Colors

As daylight wanes, hues start to fade,
A canvas bright, now softly laid.
The dance begins, the shadows play,
In twilight's embrace at the end of day.

Violet whispers creep through the dark,
While golden beams leave their gentle mark.
Crimson spills upon the green,
A symphony for sights unseen.

Brushstrokes glide in the evening air,
Painting dreams with utmost care.
Each color tells a story old,
Of love and life, in shades of gold.

In every blend, a moment caught,
The beauty found in every thought.
As day surrenders to the night,
The dance of fading colors takes flight.

So close your eyes and just believe,
In what the twilight wishes to weave.
For in this fading, beauty grows,
A dance of colors, softly flows.

The Celestial Bridge

Stars shimmer like gems, bright above,
In the quiet of night, whispers of love.
Galaxies dance, painting the sky,
A bridge of light where dreams can fly.

Clouds drift softly, molding the view,
Beneath the moon's gaze, all feels anew.
Waves of the cosmos, gentle and vast,
A promise of hope, a tether to the past.

Hearts beat in rhythm with the cosmic tune,
Echoing softly beneath the pale moon.
Connections forged through light years apart,
Infinity cradles the wandering heart.

Time stands still on this celestial path,
Guiding us gently through love's aftermath.
Each twinkle a tale, each glow a spark,
In the celestial bridge, we leave our mark.

Echoes of a Fading Sky

Crimson hues melt into the night,
Fading whispers of the day's light.
Clouds gather secrets, old and wise,
Holding the echoes of countless skies.

The sun dips low, a farewell grace,
Casting shadows, a soft embrace.
The horizon blushes, dreams awake,
With every heartbeat, the night we stake.

Stars emerge, twinkling soft and bright,
Guiding lost souls through velvet night.
Moments linger in the cooling air,
A tapestry woven with tender care.

In the silence, stories are spun,
Of lovers met and battles won.
As the sky fades, new journeys start,
In echoes of dusk, we find our heart.

A Glint of the Celestial

Amidst the dark, a glimmer breaks,
Lighting the path that hope awakes.
Twinkling fragments of distant dreams,
Illuminating all the silent screams.

The cosmos whispers, secrets unfold,
In the heart of night, tales untold.
Constellations weave stories above,
A glint of the celestial, wrapped in love.

In the hush of space, our thoughts take flight,
Carried on stardust, visions of light.
A glint shines forth, igniting our souls,
As we chase the stars, our spirit rolls.

Night cradles us in soft embrace,
While shadows dance in this timeless space.
A glint of the celestial, eternal and bright,
Guiding our hearts through the depth of night.

Silent Reverie of Dusk

In the twilight's hush, a soft retreat,
Nature's canvas, where day and night meet.
Whispers of wind through leaves cascade,
A silent reverie, memories made.

The horizon melts, colors collide,
Painting the world with a peaceful tide.
Each breath taken, a moment to pause,
In dusk's embrace, life finds its cause.

Stars shyly peek from the blanket of blue,
While shadows stretch as the evening grew.
Gold turns to gray, and dreams softly bloom,
In the silent reverie, dispersing gloom.

As night unveils her shimmering shroud,
We find our solace beneath the cloud.
With every heartbeat, the dusk weaves tight,
In the silent reverie, we find our light.

Night's Jewel-Crafted Veil

In the quiet dark, stars alight,
Whispers of dreams take graceful flight.
Moonbeams weave through shadowed trees,
A tapestry spun by night's soft breeze.

Glistening jewels on velvet skies,
Glimmers of hope in muted sighs.
Each twinkling gem, a story untold,
In the night's embrace, secrets unfold.

As the world rests in slumber's hold,
Wonders of night, both shy and bold.
Nature's symphony begins to swell,
In the hush of darkness, we find our spell.

Silhouette dances, shadows play,
Embraced by the calm, we drift away.
The night's crafted veil, serene and deep,
Cradles our thoughts, as the world sleeps.

With each passing hour, serenity reigns,
In the moon's soft glow, the spirit gains.
Night's gentle hand holds us near,
In its jewel-crafted veil, there's nothing to fear.

Shards of Light Beyond the Dusk

As day concedes to evening's haze,
Shards of light set the sky ablaze.
A canvas painted with colors rare,
Whispers of twilight dance in the air.

Purples blend with fiery gold,
Nature's palette, a sight to behold.
Hope unfurls in the dusky glow,
Promises linger where soft winds blow.

Glimmers spark in the fading light,
A farewell kiss from day to night.
Each moment captured, a fleeting grace,
In the twilight's arms, we find our place.

Shadows lengthen, the stars arise,
Night blankets the world with gentle sighs.
Within the dusk, stories arise,
Shards of light, the heart's new ties.

As darkness settles, hope remains bright,
In shards of glow, our spirits take flight.
The moment whispers; everything's alright,
In the peace of dusk, we find our light.

Luminous Trails of the Evening

As the sun dips below the tree line,
Luminous trails of gold entwine.
A pathway glows on a tranquil sea,
Guiding our hearts, wild and free.

Whispers of night call us near,
With stars above, our wishes clear.
Each step we take, a dance in time,
Luminous trails, rhythm and rhyme.

Shadows stretch, as daylight fades,
In soft twilight, our essence cascades.
Every moment, a treasure to keep,
In luminous trails, dreams gently leap.

With every breath, the night unfolds,
Magic abounds in stories told.
We follow the light where the heart has led,
On luminous trails, adventures spread.

The stars our guide in a darkened maze,
We chase the light through the evening haze.
Wanderers free, we learn to trust,
In luminous trails, ignite our lust.

The Glistening Gaze of Dim Light

In the quiet fold of the evening glow,
The glistening gaze starts to show.
Soft glimmers hush the world around,
In dim light, solace is found.

A silver sheen on the tranquil stream,
Reflections dance like a waking dream.
Each flicker tells tales of old,
In whispers of light, secrets unfold.

With every twinkle, the night awakes,
A gentle caress, the heart it shakes.
Stars wink down with a knowing smile,
In the dim light, we'll linger awhile.

Shadows play in the corners of sight,
The glistening gaze of the dim light.
Embracing the quiet, we find our way,
Fleeting moments, dusk's soft sway.

In this embrace of soft twilight,
We gather courage amid the night.
With glistening gaze, we'll brave the dark,
In the dim light's warmth, we'll leave our mark.

Twilight's Radiant Wavelengths

New colors drape the fading day,
As whispers of light softly sway.
The sun dips low, a fiery glow,
Embracing night, a quiet show.

Stars awaken in velvet skies,
Painting dreams with twinkling eyes.
Each hue tells tales of love and loss,
In twilight's warmth, we gently cross.

Gentle breezes carry the sound,
Of nature's rhythm, where peace is found.
The world slows down, a sacred pause,
Holding breath in awe for this cause.

Shadows dance on the path we tread,
As daylight yields, and dreams are fed.
In this brief moment, hearts ignite,
With hope that sparkles in the night.

Twilight's kiss sings soft and sweet,
A promise wrapped in twilight's heat.
With every shade, our spirits climb,
In radiant wavelengths, we find time.

Dazzling Shadows Unfold

Silent whispers in the night,
Where darkness shrouds with tender light.
Figures twist in the moon's embrace,
As shadows dance in a mystic space.

Every flicker hints at stories,
Of hidden hopes and ancient glories.
In the quiet, whispers grow bold,
The secrets of the night unfold.

Warmth entwined with shimm'ring grace,
Leaves a trace on a watchful face.
Though darkness reigns, there's beauty found,
In dazzling shadows all around.

Beneath the stars, all drenched in dreams,
Life's fabric weaves with silver seams.
As dawn's breath creeps to take control,
Each shadow carved, a radiant scroll.

Night may fade, but it leaves behind,
A tapestry that's sweetly entwined.
With every heartbeat, stories told,
In dazzling shadows, our lives unfold.

Flickers of Light in the Darkening Sky

As day retreats, the sky ignites,
With flickers of hope in fading lights.
Stars appear one by one, so shy,
Drawing dreams from a midnight sigh.

Moments of magic burst and fade,
In the spaces where secrets laid.
Each twinkle adds to the night's score,
A flicker's dance, and we crave more.

With whispers soft, the night reveals,
A world of wonder, where the soul heals.
Beneath the veil of darkened sky,
We gather light as the hours fly.

Every shimmer tells a tale untold,
Of distant lands and hearts of gold.
In darkness, affection lights the way,
Flickers of love in the night's ballet.

So let the night weave its gentle thread,
For in the dark, our spirits are fed.
We chase the light, though shadows pry,
Finding peace in the darkening sky.

Wisp of Light on a Gentle Breeze

With morning's breath, a wisp appears,
A beacon bright, dispelling fears.
It dances lightly on the air,
Whispering secrets without a care.

Through swaying leaves, it softly glows,
Sparking life where the wild rose grows.
A fleeting dream, a tender sigh,
Carried high where the heart can fly.

On gentle breezes, it flits and plays,
Teaching hope in the sun's warm rays.
Though brief the glimpse, it lingers sweet,
A promise wrapped in nature's beat.

Each sparkle tells of love's embrace,
A loving touch, a tranquil space.
In moments bright, our spirits rise,
A wisp of light beneath the skies.

So chase the glow, let it be known,
In every heart, a seed is sown.
With light and breezes intertwined,
We find our way, our hearts aligned.

Gentle Light of the Dimming Hour

The sun descends with grace,
Painting skies in amber hues,
Whispers of the night embrace,
As daylight softly bids adieu.

Shadows dance on golden fields,
Nature sighs, a tranquil sound,
With every fate that twilight yields,
A peaceful peace surrounds this ground.

The gentle breeze begins to flow,
Carrying secrets, old and wise,
In its embrace, we find the glow,
Of dreams ignited in the skies.

Stars awaken, twinkling bright,
In the canvas of the dark,
Guiding travelers through the night,
With their whispers, like a lark.

In this hour, as day departs,
We linger in the fading light,
Holding close the blossomed hearts,
As darkness welcomes us goodnight.

Dusk's Glittering Tapestry

Threads of gold weave through the gray,
As twilight starts to take its claim,
A woven tale of end of day,
In patterns soft, like whispered name.

Mountains wear a cloak of dusk,
As shadows stretch and softly blend,
In the air, there's a hint of musk,
Promising stories that won't end.

Whispers of the night arise,
As stars begin their playful waltz,
Painting visions across the skies,
Each twinkle holds a hidden pulse.

Amidst the trees, a hush ensues,
While crickets serenade the night,
In this realm, dreams gently fuse,
Embracing darkness with delight.

So when the day lets go of light,
And wraps the world in velvet shrouds,
We'll find our peace in endless night,
In Dusk's embrace, where hope enshrouds.

Sparkling Embrace of Nightfall

As night descends, the stars ignite,
A canvas filled with sparkling dreams,
Soft whispers echo through the night,
In tranquil tones, like gentle streams.

The moon, a lantern in the dark,
Guides wandering souls with tender care,
Illuminating each small spark,
That lingers in the midnight air.

Leaves rustle softly in the breeze,
Nature sings its lullaby sweet,
In this moment, worries cease,
As hearts unite, in rhythm beat.

A world adorned in silver light,
Where dreams take flight on whispered sighs,
In the embrace of care, so tight,
We'll weave our stories 'neath the skies.

So let us dance 'neath starlit gaze,
In nightfall's arms, we'll find our way,
In every heart, there lies a blaze,
A sparkling embrace, come what may.

The Gleam of Dusk's Caress

Glimmers rise as the day retreats,
Painting the horizon in sweet shades,
In this soft, serene release,
The world's beauty gently cascades.

A tranquil hush envelops all,
As colors blend in twilight's kiss,
In nature's beauty, we stand tall,
Finding solace in this bliss.

As shadows spread, the stars engage,
In a dance of light and dark delight,
We turn the page, a brand new stage,
Where dreams awaken in the night.

With every breath, a promise sings,
Of hope and peace that night may yield,
Wrapped in warmth, the heart takes wings,
As dusk unveils its boundless field.

So let us cherish this embrace,
This gleam that nourishes the soul,
In the caress of dusk's sweet grace,
We find our way, we are made whole.

Glimmering Horizon

The sun dips low, a painting in gold,
Waves shimmer bright, their stories unfold.
Clouds drift softly, like whispers in flight,
A glimmering horizon ignites the night.

Seas of tranquility, where peace does reside,
With every heartbeat, the world is our guide.
A journey begins with each gentle sigh,
To the glimmering horizon, we dare to fly.

The stars twinkle high, they beckon our fate,
A shimmering promise, we'll never be late.
Dancing together, as shadows extend,
On this glimmering path, our hearts shall mend.

Whispering Stars in a Fading Sky

As daylight wanes, the colors collide,
A tapestry woven, where dreams can abide.
Whispers of dusk call the stars out to play,
In a fading sky, night beckons the day.

Silence envelops, the world takes a pause,
Glimmers of hope rise, deserving applause.
Each star tells a story, a life lived in light,
In the whispering night, our hearts take flight.

We gather our wishes, like fireflies bright,
In harmony dancing, a beautiful sight.
The fading sky cradles our secrets and sighs,
With whispering stars, our spirits will rise.

The Aurora of Shadows

In the quiet of night, shadows embrace,
Painted in hues, an exquisite lace.
The aurora dances, a fleeting display,
Turning darkness to light, in a mystical way.

Whispers of secrets, the shadows unfold,
Carrying tales that the night has told.
In the twilight's arms, we find our way through,
Embraced by the colors, so vivid and true.

The aurora shines bright, a beacon so near,
Guiding our dreams, dissolving our fear.
In the embrace of shadows, we find our own ground,
Where the aurora of shadows, wraps us around.

Glistening Dreams at Sunset

The sun sets softly, a blend of warm hues,
Painting the sky with orange and blues.
Glistening dreams rise, like mist in the air,
Whispers of wishes, escaping despair.

Each moment a treasure, a promise to keep,
Held in the twilight, where silence runs deep.
Dreams glimmer like stars, as night takes its hold,
In the beauty of sunset, our spirits unfold.

We chase after moments, that spark in our soul,
In glistening dreams, we find ourselves whole.
As the sunset fades, our hearts start to soar,
Glistening dreams at sunset, forevermore.

Nightfall's Caress

The sun dips low, shadows creep,
Whispers of night begin to seep.
Stars awaken, one by one,
In the twilight, day is done.

Moonlight spills on quiet streets,
A soft embrace, the night retreats.
Crickets sing a lullaby sweet,
As dreams and dusk together meet.

The world adorned in silver hue,
A gentle veil, a mystic view.
Trees sway lightly in the breeze,
Nature sighs, the heart finds ease.

In the stillness, moments pause,
Thoughts wander, without a cause.
The dark enfolds like velvet deep,
Nightfall's caress, a secret to keep.

Beneath the stars, our hopes ignite,
A canvas painted with pure light.
Embrace the night, the soft regret,
For dawn will come, but not just yet.

The Hidden Glow

In a garden where the shadows play,
Flowers bloom in a secret way.
Petals glisten under the moon,
Their hidden glow sings a tune.

Whispers dance upon the air,
A fragrance lingers, light as prayer.
In this quiet, magic swells,
Tales of wonder time compels.

A breeze sweeps through the ancient trees,
Carrying laughter, soft as keys.
In the stillness, hearts take flight,
Finding solace in the night.

Stars above, like lanterns bright,
Guide the lost with gentle light.
In the dark, stories unfold,
The hidden glow, a warmth retold.

Silent moments, dreams we sow,
In the night, we truly grow.
Embrace the mystery, let it flow,
Life's sweetest joys, in the hidden glow.

Shimmering Dusk

Golden rays spill from the west,
As day bids night a gentle rest.
Clouds adorned with amber lace,
A world transformed in twilight's grace.

Birds return to their cozy nests,
The sky ablaze, nature's best.
As colors blend, the shadows play,
Shimmering dusk, a fleeting ballet.

The horizon glows with promise bright,
As the stars blink in delight.
A lullaby of evening songs,
In this moment, all belongs.

Whispers of night brush past my ear,
The silence speaks, as if to hear.
A tranquil pause, a heart laid bare,
In the beauty of shimmering air.

As darkness falls, the glow persists,
A tapestry of midnight twists.
Hold the magic, let it stay,
For shimmering dusk guides the way.

Glistening Veils of Evening

The sun descends behind the hills,
A quiet hush, the world instills.
Veils of twilight softly unfurl,
As night begins to gently whirl.

Stars awaken, diamond bright,
Each twinkle holds a wish in flight.
Moonbeams paint the earth below,
In glistening veils, the night will glow.

The whispers of the evening breeze,
Carry secrets through the trees.
In the stillness, time stands still,
A heart finds peace, a sacred thrill.

Cool shadows stretch on the ground,
In this magic, love is found.
With every breath, the moments blend,
In glistening veils, the night will mend.

So close your eyes and drift away,
Let the stars guide you where they may.
In the calm, our dreams take flight,
Wrapped in glistening veils of night.

Shadows drenched in Elysian Glow

In twilight's grace we roam so free,
Beneath a sky of dreams to be.
The whispers of the night take flight,
While shadows dance with soft delight.

A river flows with silver gleam,
As stars ignite the night's sweet theme.
Elysian notes in air do swell,
In quiet corners where we dwell.

Moonlit paths that gently tread,
With every word that goes unsaid.
We linger where the soft winds blow,
In shadows drenched in Elysian glow.

Within the dusk our secrets blend,
Where moments pause and love transcends.
A fleeting kiss, the world in hush,
In this serene and sacred brush.

So here we stand, hearts intertwined,
In gentle waves, our souls aligned.
Each star above a vow we weave,
In shadows' glow, we dare believe.

Twilight's Gilded Reverie

Amid the dusk, a palette bright,
Where day and dusk converge in light.
The sky adorned with shades anew,
In twilight's arms, a world to view.

Golden hues on leaves cascade,
A fleeting dance that will not fade.
With every breath, the magic sighs,
As dreams awaken in our eyes.

The whispers of the closing day,
In gilded traces softly sway.
A moment held, a promise made,
In twilight's glow, our dreams won't fray.

Each heartbeat soft, a sonnet sweet,
Where echoes of the past we meet.
With every glance, a world unfolds,
In twilight's gaze, our story holds.

So let us wander, hand in hand,
Through painted skies, a promised land.
Forever wrapped in evening's lace,
In twilight's gilded, warm embrace.

Evanescent Gleams beneath the Stars

In stillness finds a moment's grace,
Where time dissolves in night's embrace.
Evanescent gleams will spark,
Beneath the cosmos, soft and dark.

A whisper flows, celestial tide,
With secrets of the night to bide.
Each twinkle tells of distant dreams,
In silvered light, our spirit gleams.

The universe in dance tonight,
As constellations guide our flight.
With open hearts, we learn to see,
The beauty in tranquility.

For every star that fades away,
A memory begins to sway.
In moments pure as starlight beams,
We weave our hopes, we chase our dreams.

Together lost in cosmic lore,
We hold the night and seek for more.
In evanescent gleams we trust,
Beneath the stars, our hearts are just.

The Iridescent Horizon

Where sky and sea in colors blend,
The horizon calls, a journey's end.
Iridescent waves embrace the shore,
As whispers of the breeze implore.

Each dawn awakens dreams anew,
In shades of pink and vibrant blue.
With every rise, the sun's first gleam,
Ignites the world, a brilliant dream.

We chase the light with open hearts,
In nature's art, where each day starts.
The horizon's kiss, a golden trace,
Guides us forth in life's grand race.

As twilight gathers, colors soar,
We find our place upon the shore.
The evening glows, a moment's sigh,
In iridescence, we learn to fly.

Together we will face the sky,
With each horizon, we'll rise high.
For in the light of day's decline,
The iridescent paths entwine.

Radiance at Dusk

The sun dips low, a golden sigh,
Colors blend in the evening sky.
Whispers of night begin to creep,
As day surrenders, the world in sleep.

Shadows stretch on the emerald ground,
In this quiet, a peace is found.
Crickets sing their evening tune,
While stars awaken, one by one, soon.

Moonlight dances on waves so bright,
Guiding dreams through the velvet night.
A canvas painted in hues so deep,
Nature's secrets in silence keep.

The horizon glows with a final flare,
Promises whispered in the cool night air.
Each moment cherished, time held tight,
In the embrace of the coming night.

As radiance fades, hearts align,
In the twilight, all souls intertwine.
The world transformed, so serene,
In the dusk's gentle, warm sheen.

Celestial Reflections

Above the world, a vast expanse,
Where dreams and stars do dance.
Silver lanterns shine so bright,
Guiding wanderers through the night.

Each twinkle tells a timeless tale,
Of cosmic winds and comet's trail.
In the dark, hope starts to rise,
Mirrored in the endless skies.

Softly glows the milky way,
Stitching night into the day.
Galaxies swirl in silent grace,
In this infinite, open space.

As we gaze, we're swept away,
Lost in the magic of the astral sway.
Thoughts take flight like shooting stars,
Connecting hearts, no matter how far.

Celestial bodies watch and wait,
Holding secrets of love and fate.
In their glow, we find our place,
Reflections of the human race.

Shards of the Dimming Light

The sun descends with a soft goodbye,
Casting diamonds on the evening sky.
Fragments of warmth begin to fade,
As darkness steals the daylight's shade.

In the twilight, colors intertwine,
Flickering voices in the pine.
The world, a canvas of soft retreat,
Where day and night joyfully meet.

Flecks of gold, a transient flare,
Haunting whispers linger in the air.
Each ray, a memory left behind,
A gentle brush that binds the mind.

The horizon drinks the last of the sun,
As shadows meld, and day is done.
Stars break through with their silver light,
Threads of hope in the fabric of night.

Shards of the dimming light reflect,
A tapestry where dreams connect.
In this hush of the waning day,
The heart learns to find its way.

A Tapestry of Stars

In the velvet hush of the deep night,
Stars weave stories, shimmering bright.
Each twinkle, a thread in the cosmic seam,
Together they gather, like a shared dream.

Constellations draw maps of old,
With legends and myths in their fold.
The sky adorned with a jeweled crown,
An infinite quilt that can never drown.

Guided by light from millions of years,
We stir in wonder, release our fears.
Galaxies swirl in a grand ballet,
Whispering secrets that never decay.

In the quiet of night, we find our place,
Amidst the wonders of boundless space.
Hearts ignited by the celestial dance,
In the tapestry of stars, we take a chance.

A moment suspended in the cosmic flow,
Connecting us all in the softest glow.
Beneath this sky, we dream, ignite,
Together we flourish, in the depths of night.

Fading Colors

The sunset whispers quiet sighs,
As hues of orange softly die.
In shadows deep, where silence lies,
The day retreats, as night draws nigh.

Once vibrant leaves now gently fall,
They dance with grace, then lose it all.
A tapestry begins to stall,
As nature answers autumn's call.

The skies grow dim, the stars appear,
A fading glow that brings a tear.
Yet in this loss, we hold so dear,
A memory forged, forever near.

With every breath, we find the grace,
In fleeting moments, time we face.
For colors fade, yet leave a trace,
A story told in nature's space.

So let us cherish what we see,
In fading light, we find the key.
For though it ends, so joyfully,
In every loss, there's beauty free.

Radiant Souls

Within the heart, a spark ignites,
A flame that dances, pure and bright.
In every smile, a world delights,
Radiant souls shine through the night.

With laughter shared, connections grow,
In simple acts, the love will flow.
Through kindness sown, we start to know,
The warmth that life's true gifts bestow.

Rejected dreams may cast a pall,
Yet hope will rise, and we won't fall.
In shadows deep, we'll heed the call,
With radiant light, we stand so tall.

Through storms we weather, hand in hand,
Together strong, our hearts have planned.
In unity, our voices strand,
A symphony across the land.

So shine your light, let spirits soar,
In every soul, there's so much more.
Embrace the love that we explore,
A journey vast, forevermore.

A Symphony of Glimmers

In twilight's hush, a soft refrain,
The stars emerge, a bright domain.
Each twinkle sings, dispelling pain,
A symphony composed in vain.

With every heartbeat, dreams align,
As constellations start to shine.
In cosmic dance, we find a sign,
Through melodies of space, divine.

The moonlight filters, gentle grace,
Each glimmer finds its rightful place.
In shadows deep, we trace the face,
Of stories told in time and space.

The night unfolds, a canvas wide,
With dreams and wishes side by side.
In silent whispers, hopes abide,
A harmony we cannot hide.

So close your eyes, and feel the call,
The symphony that binds us all.
For in this night, we rise, we fall,
A luminous tale through stars enthrall.

Celestial Kaleidoscope at Night

A canvas vast, the night unfolds,
With colors brushed in hues so bold.
The cosmos spins, a tale retold,
A kaleidoscope of dreams we hold.

Through swirling lights, the dreams take flight,
In every star, a spark of light.
The night transforms in sheer delight,
As galaxies dance, a wondrous sight.

In whispers soft, the cosmos sighs,
As constellations weave their ties.
With every glance, imagination flies,
In celestial hearts, a truth complies.

The heavens pulse with cosmic song,
Where every note feels like belonging.
A symphony that calls us strong,
In endless beauty, we find where we belong.

So look above, and let dreams soar,
In this kaleidoscope, explore.
For night's embrace brings hope galore,
A universe of wonders, evermore.

Laughter of the Flickering Stars

In midnight's glow, a laughter weaves,
As flickering stars hum sweet reprieves.
In cosmic play, the heart believes,
A merry dance, the soul receives.

They twinkle bright like secrets shared,
In every wink, the night is bared.
With gleeful beams, they always dared,
To light the dark, our hopes declared.

The moon joins in with gentle chime,
As laughter echoes through the time.
A melody, a joyful rhyme,
In sparkling eyes, the stars align.

So let us raise our voices clear,
In celebration, far and near.
For in this night, there's nothing to fear,
With laughter lit, our hearts adhere.

Together in this cosmic spree,
With flickering stars, we're wild and free.
In timeless grace, eternally,
The laughter of the stars, our glee.

Opalescent Veil of the Night

Beneath the silvered sky, we dwell,
Whispers of shadows, a soft-spoken bell,
Stars twinkle gently, secrets in flight,
Wrapped in the opalescent veil of the night.

Moonbeams dance lightly upon the ground,
A symphony of silence, where dreams resound,
Each glimmering essence, a story untold,
In the embrace of the night, hearts unfold.

Through misty horizons, our wishes take wing,
Caught in the stillness, the nightbird will sing,
Ghosts of the past weave their patterns so bright,
Under the tender, opalescent light.

Eternity lingers within every glance,
Moments in time weave a shimmering trance,
Guided by starlight, we journey so right,
Lost in the folds of the opalescent night.

Faltering Light

In the dimming glow of the fading sun,
Shadows grow tall, the day's nearly done,
Whispers of twilight in colors so bright,
Paint the horizon with faltering light.

Leaves rustle softly in the gentle breeze,
Echoes of laughter dance through the trees,
Moments of magic in fleeting delight,
Chasing the remnants of faltering light.

The world holds its breath as the darkness calls,
Painting the canvas where evening falls,
Beneath the stars, we gather the night,
Cradled in dreams of the faltering light.

Each flicker a promise, each shadow a tale,
Guiding the wanderers who seek not to fail,
A journey awaits where hope is ignited,
Under the sky where the light has retreated.

Untold Dreams

In the garden of thoughts where whispers reside,
Untold dreams gather, with nowhere to hide,
Perfumed with longing, they take to the skies,
Painting a world where the heart never lies.

Moments unfold like petals in bloom,
Each brings a promise, dispelling the gloom,
Woven together by forces unseen,
Carried by currents of all that has been.

Where echoes of laughter and shadows entwine,
Secrets of time in the stars brightly shine,
Casting their glow on the paths that we tread,
Leading us onward through dreams never said.

In silence, they beckon, in midnight's embrace,
Chasing horizons, a leap through the space,
Untamed yet tender, like whispers from streams,
Guiding the souls to their untold dreams.

The Gleam of Wandering Souls

Beneath a sky of inky black lace,
Meandering stars leave a wistful trace,
Each flicker a compass, leading the way,
To the gleam of wandering souls at play.

In stillness, they dance through the veil of the night,
Gathering stories, igniting the light,
Threads of existence, entwined in their flight,
A tapestry woven with shadows so bright.

Whispers of hope in the cool midnight hush,
Moving like rivers, in silent, sweet rush,
They carry the wishes of those who have roamed,
Finding their way, in the gleam they call home.

Echoing laughter in the spaces between,
They craft a communion, a sight so serene,
Wandering freely through realms yet unknown,
The light in their hearts, forever their own.

Starlit Serenity

In the cradle of night, a hush descends,
Stars offer solace as daylight ends,
Each twinkle a promise, each shimmer a sigh,
In the realm of starlit serenity, we lie.

The moon softly whispers, a lullaby sweet,
Crickets keep rhythm, their song is complete,
Wrapped in the stillness, all worries take flight,
Beneath the vast canopy, love feels so right.

We breathe in the magic that dances around,
Finding our place where true peace can be found,
Caught in the moments, the world falls away,
In starlit serenity, we choose to stay.

Hearts pulse in harmony, dreams come alive,
Bathed in the glow where the endless stars dive,
Each flicker a memory that time can't erase,
In the arms of serenity, we find our place.

Milton Keynes UK
Ingram Content Group UK Ltd.
UKHW010229111224
452348UK00011B/616